A FINITUDE OF SKIN

Clayton Adam Clark

Moon City Press

MOON CITY PRESS
Department of English
Missouri State University
901 South National Avenue
Springfield, Missouri 65897

The narratives contained herein are works of fiction. All incidents, situations, institutions, governments, and people are fictional, and any similarity to characters or persons living or dead is strictly coincidental.

Library of Congress Cataloging-in-Publication Data

Clark, Clayton Adam
A Finitude of Skin: poems/Clayton Adam Clark, 1983–

2018958388

Further Library of Congress information is available upon request.

ISBN-10: 0-913785-74-1
ISBN-13: 978-0-913785-74-4

Cover and interior illustrated and designed by Charli Barnes
Author photo by Tina Cummings
Edited by Karen Craigo

Manufactured in the United States of America.

www.mooncitypress.com

Acknowledgments

Thank you to Michael Czyzniejewski, Lanette Cadle, Karen Craigo, Charli Barnes, and the rest of the team at Moon City Press for their incredible support in bringing this book into the world. What an honor. I am also grateful to the editors at magazines who gave some of these poems their first lives on a printed page or screen. And I am humbled by the gifted poets who offered insight and praise for this book, including Andrew Hudgins, Wyatt Prunty, Lo Kwa Mei-en, Travis Mossotti, and Matthew Sumpter.

I am grateful to and fond of my professors at Ohio State, especially the poets Andrew Hudgins, Henri Cole, and Kathy Fagan, whose workshop voices are still in my head when I sit down to write. In particular, I am thankful to Andrew, who not only taught me to write in meter and tell a joke, but has continued to be a tremendous mentor and friend. Special thanks, too, to Michelle Herman, Lee Martin, Erin McGraw, Lee K. Abbott, and Jennifer Schlueter for their kindness and guidance, both in the classroom and out. My three years in Columbus were good ones, to say the least.

Thank you to my creative writing professors at DePauw for bearing with me as I attempted those first poems, stories, and essays: Joseph Heithaus, Peter Graham, Barbara Bean, Chris White, and Greg Schwipps. I'm not sure I could have ended up here without your (patient) early encouragement.

A rowdy and loving thank you to my OSU compatriots, especially Bill Riley, Gabriel Urza, Derek Palacio, Alex Streiff, Daniel Carter, Claire Vaye Watkins, Isaac Anderson, Matthew Sumpter, and my poet cohort: James Ellenberger, Lo Kwa Mei-en, Benjamin Glass, Allison Pitinii Davis, and Tory Adkisson. I feel fortunate to have studied with you then and continue to be thrilled to read your literary accomplishments now.

Friends, family, parents, and brothers—near and far, old and new—I take it you know who you are. Thank you for everything. I hope you'll see and feel the influence you've had on me returning to you in these words.

And finally, I'm so thankful to Tina, whose love, support, patience, and friendship have, indeed, been "above average."

Grateful acknowledgement is made to editors at the journals where these poems first appeared:

Bellingham Review: "The Laws of Motion"

Birmingham Poetry Review: "Salvage: A Field Guide"

The Carolina Quarterly: "Zygo-"

Cimarron Review: "Exposure Being: A Letter"

Cottonwood: "Bones, Granite, Dirt, and Brains: A Soteriology"

Fourteen Hills: "The Winter Litany"

Harpur Palate: "Seed Tick: A Palimpsest" and "The Elephant Rocks"

Lake Effect: "Nonunion"

The Massachusetts Review: "Self-Portrait With Asian Carp and Mississippi"

Meridian: "Warehouse Staining"

Mid-American Review: "The Noctambulists"

Moon City Review: "Ouroboric"

New Madrid: A Journal of Contemporary Literature: "Invasive Species: An Epithalamion" and "Leach"

Passages North: "Skeleton"

Potomac Review: "Febrile"

The Southeast Review: "The River of Ugly Fishes," "Bagworms and Blood Vessels," and "Cadaver Worlds"

Southern California Review: "Transference"

Southern Humanities Review: "Self-Portrait with Wasp and Weather"

Spoon River Poetry Review: "Wind Farm"

Thin Air Magazine: "Winter Skin"

Verse Daily: "The River of Ugly Fishes"

Washington Square Magazine: "Shape-Shifter"

Zone 3: "Self-Portrait with Fescue and Dogwood"

Table of Contents

A FINITUDE OF SKIN

I.

The River of Ugly Fishes

Blame it on the limestone—the sinkholes,
the speleological interest, an overwhelming
karstness here. People get lost.
Its tributaries are losing, but a hellbender
of Eastern origin has shown its face
this far west. The snot otter, grampus,
devil dog can breathe underwater
without gills, lungs only for floating,
and most closely resembles crayfish-eating
petrified wood. Until it swims. The limestone
swallows water, cuts down the streams,
and thus this river, but filters mud
like a sieve. Water goes in—it must
come out—mud never leaves. The color
of muddy river, there's nothing wooden
in a hellbender's wiggle-work upstream,
the backbone soft, the little flesh around
infused with capillaries that filter
oxygen. A spring, the state's fifth largest,
restores groundwater to air. Rock gives
and takes, erodes, but water does
what it pleases, like two-foot salamanders
with no known predators except for humans
camping along these banks. One tripped in
a hole—the underground cave beneath
collapsed. It died. Blame the bedrock,
permeable and hollow. It follows water
all places, for water is strong willed—
this land is weak. Or blame the ocean
that left for deeper chasms instead
of limestone, the compressed remains
of creatures who swam here, dying
for karst, so long before Missouri.

Skeleton

After they sewed him up, the surgeons
told my friend, *Your spine was spongy*

enough to cut with a butter knife.
That stuck with me, like patients who come to

with gauze packed beneath stitches, but I didn't
present it until I was eating fried Oreos

at the state fair and admiring butter
carved into a cow. *I could've built a replica*

of Matt's skeleton, I thought, *and won first prize,*
only I'd cast it in plaster afterward

to remember it beyond the butter's melting.
The cast could double as a coat rack

or a floor lamp, a light bulb stemming
from each vertebra to make it practical,

unlike a degenerating spine. Still, it's hard
to believe. When my mother was pitched

through a windshield, she left her hair
and skin from her calves and shoulder blades

on the pavement she slid across. The EMTs
transported her on a backboard, she slept

two weeks in a coma and lost her name
and everything for a while, but she didn't break

a single bone. When I think it's unfair,
what happened to her and Matt, I track down

why that's true. I name the bones, trace them
from anywhere up to my skull to prove all things

connect, like cause and effect, which is tough
because of the gaps between. Without them

I'm arthritic, but I want the pieces
to work as one like the radius I broke

playing soccer. The weight's too much
sometimes, my forearm popping in bright

flashbulbs of pain when I torque it wrong
at the fuse site. Unthinking, I bear it

to my sternum and nurse it there, just one
slow-curving rib away from my backbone.

Warehouse Staining

Black fungus climbs the corrugated metal,
and scorched white-oak barrels yield sugars
to their loads within. Stacked hundreds of feet high,
ten thousand years of bourbon casts off water
and alcohol waste, feeding a fungus lacking green

enough to eat the sun. Does it lay siege
to the warehouse or swell out from the core—
thinning airborne ethanol like a liver as it rushes
nearby hills and trees, the homes in dusky scabs?
Livers can be lobed and given—a fifth

of a brain-dead adult's will grow inside
and with a child. Is it surprising what can be
lived on and where it's gotten? The seer
swears the futures of new vessels lie
in origins, but to grow back on the dregs

of another is not regeneration. All reuse waste
in souring age, and mushrooms are only fruit
from quiet fungi eating the soil. Were the fungus
living on what's exhaled through the staves
of every barrel a threat, they'd treat the growth

to protect such purposeful aging. There'd be a man
working atop steel scaffolding who showered
metal walls with chemicals—a man who toiled
to erase or restrain this birthmark or colony—
and none of the gorgeous warehouse stains.

Bagworms and Blood Vessels

Silk-knotted to the juniper bushes,
bagworms hung camouflaged by dead

scale leaves in front of our mother's house.
To preserve the flora, we had to poison

or pluck the bags after summer and before
the eggs hatched in spring. It was fall

when I closed my eyes against the sun,
its red strobing behind my eyelids,

and knew that I would die by now. Instead,
you almost did. The cavernoma, a raspberry

of blood vessels blown out but not broken,
played havoc with the quiet voltaic needs

of your temporal lobe, but a dozen seizures
were all we could see of the flaw inside

your skull. Like the above-ground pool,
that mosquito breeding ground where grass

wouldn't grow after Mom made us tear it down,
my premonition remains vivid, though not

useful. Spitting-image Brother, maybe
I mistook you for me. Tell me, what's seizure

taste like? In case our brains have formed as much
alike as our faces, prepare me for the lucid,

visionless paralysis. Bag-bound and wingless,
the female bagworm vacates her home in fall

after it's full with eggs to die. Her larvae seize
it for their own—in seizure you have no control.

I once saw you fall on a horseshoe stake,
your sternum underpinned by rusted metal,

and like now, no blood deserted your body
nor could I do more than hope you breathed.

No one's wholly distinct, yet each must see
his body through. After enough generations,

the bagworms brought defoliated death
upon their host, and the juniper's yellowing

rot in front of our childhood home was all
I noticed, not a familial ebb and flow of worms.

Cadaver Worlds

A curation of plastinated flesh, the human
bodies were poised for a perpetual wake.
Parents and kids stared, crowding around a brain

cross-sectioned, smoker's lungs, the hurdler's

testicles. If this is the new circus, I'm its freak,
stabled by a garbage can and swallowing back
hot, pre-puke saliva. *What's wrong with me?*

I read the philosophy on the walls—*Don't stop*

breathing—but couldn't ignore the flayed man
upholding the rumpled quilt of his own skin.
I can't not fathom all that's concealed inside

my largest organ. If we must assign superlatives,

morphology dictates brains, encased in bone,
most vital—then caged hearts. I once got to
watch a dead man donate his heart valves.

The technicians covered his face and genitals

with towels before they cut a U into his chest.
His skin and yellow subcutaneous fat clamped
away from the incision, they pinched through

each rib with pliers. The sound of a live tree branch

breaking and breaking. I hovered near the trash—
they unfettered a heart from pericardium
and major blood vessels. *You can't stop breathing.*

Removed from its body, the heart is more

abstract and less. I excused myself as they began
on the back skin with a dermatome, but the people-
cutting people swore you learn to get used to it.

Self-Portrait with Wasp and Weather

It's rained for days. Each collision of body
and window vibrates briefly as the word *dint*

before the wasp secures flight from free fall.
Taking another turn of my living room,

the insect wields its mass-times-velocity
against the triple-pane, which is like racing

a motorcycle into a brick wall, an exoskeleton
the nearest any come to indestructible.

A hurricane with a biblical name has struck
the Gulf and broadcasts rain six hundred miles

up the Mississippi. Crucial viscera concealed
within armor thirst if the wasp lies down

on the windowsill before consuming nectar.
When the outer fibers embrittle, its body curls

a tiny C. Low-pressure systems spiral
counterclockwise, and humans can lack

water a few days before blood thickens
and kidneys fail. Postmortem caloricity,

the cells burning through the last resources
after the organs shut down, is the bonfire

mounted once a city's sacked, the furniture
and dead piled up, or so I can imagine

because my skull is human body armor
that shields the water in and sunlight out.

The news exhibits people with dogs on roofs
of their half-submerged Delta homes.

This is as close as I get. I open the door—
it's rained so much it no longer smells like rain.

On TV, people man johnboats to rescue
others from roofs, and might I send money

to save them—-or the pets? Wasps have stung me,
but I don't kill all wasps; people have helped me,

but I can't help these people. We've all a thorax
and maybe a wood-pulp nest where sympathy can

unwind with a glass of water, where pliant skin
cells slough their dead and brain cells formulate

contingency plans. My city's river floods.
The hurricane has begotten tornados, the news

reports, though I heard sirens an hour ago.
That I'm endangered despite my comforts

is hardly new. At home or seeking it,
loyal cells stand ready to burn me down.

From Our Leaflike Capillaries

Osmotic, possums in the alley trash,
heels thudding on hardwood floors,

and a crescendo of female moans
seep through the apartment walls

and our tympanic membranes. We retreat
to the dusk on our deck, where I grill fish

and you drink wine and we watch the bats
flit for mosquitoes in the alley. They course by

privacy fences and dodge the power lines
to eat that which would eat us while we eat.

When the wind blows our way, we smell
fumes a sewer grate exhausts beyond

our fence line, and for a week, it stank
of wet fur—a dog or maybe drowned

possum. A train shrieks on the south side
where the Mississippi River accepts

the volume of the Meramec. That filthy,
north-flowing river—we used to float it

each summer, drinking and canoeing past
water-damaged homes. Dehydrated and sunburnt,

we returned to camp, and I followed you
back to our tent. I zipped it shut

behind us. I dropped my suit and pulled
your bikini strings. On the tarpaulin floor

where we could feel rocks and tufts of grass
beneath, we both went quiet to keep our sex

inside the nylon. We hid our skin
in the sleeping bag and slept till dinner,

but from our leaflike capillaries
female mosquitoes fed, their timbre

the theophonic we can't hear, then can,
then don't as the proboscis injects saliva.

We woke with histamine in our blood,
the wheals already dotting our throats

and faces, while the constellation of insects
across our tent ceiling quietly digested

what was once us to synthesize their young.

Invasive Species: An Epithalamion

Koi surfacing between lily pads bothered
nothing in the pond by where we married
except insects that touched down on the water,

but brocaded carp will plague someplace
not manmade. Rooting substrate for food,
koi silt the water, challenging the traditions

of native species to hunt and photosynthesize.
Plus, their sheen subsides in a few generations
to match the mud. Just as the Mississippi

leans into Illinois, yielding more Missouri,
the markers that distinguish bodies mutate
with time. You and I are much the same

in DNA and the microbiota in our guts,
so we've shared life. Something in the way
bull sharks regulate salt in their bloodstream,

they can rove upriver past brackish water.
Fishermen hooked one on the Illinois side,
thirteen hundred miles from saltwater

and most of its kind. One bull shark amasses
more press than schools of carp killing schools
and schools of other fish, but it is small

organisms, the microflora traveling between us,
that thrive. Ninety percent of cells on my body
aren't human and sixty percent of me is water—

I'm uncertain what you see in me
is even me. But my vow, *I'm with you,*
transfigures me into the ecosystem you inhabit

without competition because when our matter
changes cell by cell every ten years,
we can't commit our bodies long.

The Winter Litany

Tire tread on the highway across
the river, its friction magnified
by rain, intrudes upon this bedroom

where two breathe each other's
carbon dioxide beneath the covers.

When a body's mostly one coiled tube,
sharing excretions is a romantic thing.
Out back, at least two cats share

the space beneath the stoop this winter,
cohabitation a luxury and need.

Car sounds and wind work past the storm
windows and then the double-pane
loose in its frame. Plastic sheets

the couple taped to the frames keep in
their heat, their exhalations, but cleave

wind from the sound of spinning, wet
rubber. Mice live beneath the refrigerator—
warm coils below cold food, beer,

and far above, meat in the freezer.
Stray cats outside and the mice scour

floors and countertops. Wind stretches
the plastic sheets against their tape,
aching to evict the heat within.

The man wakes to displace the beers
from dinner, but his arm still sleeps,

is heaviest when the muscles are a burden.
He squeezes his fist till the nerves wake
and the vessels fill and the arm grows

denser but lighter, too. Cats probably
don't expel their meager winter waste

inside their shelter. The mice, however, do,
the couple finds in spring when the man walks
the refrigerator out from the wall to scrub

the floor. They tear down the sheets
of insulation and open windows to free

a season's air. They set traps, though
the mice have left. The couple cleans
around and with each other, like old

dancers who know each other's bodies
but never see their peculiar grace for lack

of mirrors: he unscrews the light fixture
above their bed, she sweeps the dead
ladybugs it held into the trash can.

II.

Seed Tick: A Palimpsest

Our state issued a policy of executing inmates
with straight pentobarbital, same as vets
putting down sick dogs. Unable to keep oxygen-
rich blood in its brain, our dog would pass out
from excitement, the vet blaming these anoxic
events on nodes that mushroomed from each
failing organ. To the end I'd like to remain
useful to you, but given my family history
of apoplexy, let's not count on it. If when
you can no longer see my name in this body
they still won't let a person choose his end,
please leave me. It's the time of year
for accidental deaths. A boy drowned last summer,
and boaters found his body surfaced miles
downriver. The parents tried to donate his organs
and tissues, but waterlogged cells are helpful
to no one. So give what you can then burn
me down and dump the dust into a river
because you know how much I've tried to be
everything to everyone. Remember the time
we saw a bull elk ahead on the hiking path?
You dashed downhill, and I followed you across
the bottoms to a riverbank. Crouched among
sawtoothed boulders, we listened through the water
roiling behind us, but all that ever tried to hurt us
were seed ticks we found crawling up our shoes,
heedless of the poison we'd sprayed on our legs.

Leach

We moored our canoe beside the cave. After we lowered
our bodies into the spring pool, the earth-cold water sapped

heat from my wife and me, our hearts sedated and blood
vessels constricted, while our brains throbbed with acuity.

Springs are caves that void water, and climacteric to water
humans drink, the cave's a state-protected geologic form.

But the law's murky: If a man owns a tract of southern Missouri
and finds hollowed dolomite beneath his Menfro soil, he owns

and might have the right to foul it. And if he dumps railroad ties
in the woods above that cave, creosote that seeps into the dirt

will spoil the cave's pH, killing its eyeless, pellucid fauna.
Acclimated to fifty-five degrees and a steady influx of unsoiled water,

life there is vulnerable to disruption. The man with a pistol,
waiting where his land bordered the river, was disturbed

by a young man who'd stopped his canoe to piss in the weeds.
The bullet that entered his face welcomed blood out

onto the limestone, and the question in a stand-your-ground state
is does the gunman's property line extend to the river's edge

where the blood seeped. Here's another one: Is the blood
now the gunman's? After we lifted ourselves from the gelid pool,

my wife and I warmed our bodies upstream in the muddied
green river like the sun-loving animals we are, our red blood

restoring the outer reaches of our flesh. We never trespassed
inside the cave. For a long time now, we've been digging a hole

in the earth and backfilling it with a body minus its fluids,
organs, and anything wet enough to provoke decomposition

before a wake, plus three gallons of embalming fluid or however
much is needed to forestall the thoracic cavity's wont to cave.

Febrile

A house centipede darts the baseboard
by my side of the bed, and with lymph nodes
swollen like stone fruit beneath my jaw,
I drink from the water jug and pass you it.
What's mine is yours includes this virus,
all the nucleic acids we've shared in this bed,
so our hypothalami turn up the heat,
burning cells dry, and we layer on clothes.
The body's desiderata of warmth and water
convene us. I watch the centipede crawl
upon the husk of one of its species but can't
see what takes place between the living
and dead. It's easy to forget our bodies
are sacs we must keep full with water,
the skin a sieve and no less permeable
than these cotton sweatshirts. Our DNA
breaks down at 284 degrees—the helix unwinds
in dehydration. Here, drink more water.
Pressed from our pores, whatever salt was you
or me may coalesce in the solitary blanket
of dead skin coating our bed. You have to sweat
your body out alone, but we can be more
resilient. We can make each other comfortable.
I've turned the electric blanket on high as it goes.

The Laws of Motion

I.

We wiped the closet ceiling with bleach water,
and the mold paled. You edged and I rolled on
ultra-white paint, and we praised our success
too soon—green-black crop circles emerged
later that week. We learned to destroy first
the source of moisture. Waiting for men
who tuck-pointed our decomposing mortar,
we researched the spores, their precarious urge
to float and take up residence in our lungs.
Mold either succumbs to the animal's resistance
or kills its host then dies—the dying patient,
though most tolerate anything for its deferral.
A teenager spelunking Missouri caves breathed
the fungus that eats bat droppings and died
from histoplasmosis. But his leukemia
was in remission, so immunocompetent,
we may be all right. We grow hardier
with repeat exposure to microflora, but
remission's a disease asleep and much still
agitates the dormant. We'll stay alert. This time
we armored ourselves in masks and latex gloves
when we killed the fungus growing in our house.

II.

Sweetgums loose wicked seeds that clot
our sunburnt grass. The year we couldn't shoot
fireworks for lack of rain, the basement walls
dehisced in autumn,
                rain impressing through
concrete pores and sloping toward the drain.
Don't ask what this means for our foundation.
I try not to
                think of brown recluses, their autumn
exile to warm, moist homes.
                     You and your bugs,
you said, but I found one in our bedroom
and replied, *I knew a guy who lost a chunk*

of forehead to a bite. You went to sleep
while I sprayed toxins where wall and floor
converged,
                second story to basement, and soaked
our thresholds. Dead leaves on the carpet
triggered double takes, and I stirred up
basement storage—the rakes for scratching

gumballs from our lawn—to scare out fiddlebacks.
I killed one, but can there be just one?
                     Reclusa—
some spiders pose as venomous. That night I woke,
already standing, from a dream of spiders
in our bed. I ripped back the covers and yelled,

though even as you fled—*What? Where is it?*—
I suspected the violin
                spiders an echo snared
in my skull. Panic is a communicable disease.
        Like a plumb bob tapped into swing,
the next winter's the coldest of our lives.

After a night out, you ran upstairs, stripped,
and warmed
            your lower half in the bathtub.
I rolled my pant legs and sat on the ledge
behind you, submerging
                        my ischemic feet,
a near-necrosis. Our capillaries admitted

blood again. The next day you showed me
oval bruises
            that colored the tips of your toes,
as though the return of blood had been too stark,
the farthest vessels from your heart now ruptured.

III.

Two air movements, one a cold front,
the other warm, collided, abusing the aged

sycamores in our park. The city dispatched
men to chainsaw the fallen trunks

of hundred-year-old trees into rutted cylinders,
then grind them down to mulch for bedding

the saplings. No thing recedes—it persists
elsewhere—but I feel me slowing down.

At twenty, we parked most nights in a park
overlooking the Meramec's floodplain—

the hillside bequeathed by a man who built
landscaping machines—and fooled around

in back, exerting gambits around our bodies'
mathematics. We got busted once, perhaps

the night that nights first start to lengthen
and the soybeans launch into reproduction.

*No, Officer, we didn't drink this summer
solstice.* I was later stopped by a possum

while jogging near our first home. A standoff
beneath a streetlamp—we didn't vocalize,

but in running opposite ways we confessed
to a shared interest. Measured against near-level

stacks of brick, a possum is as wild as we get,
yet it thrives so long as it avoids people and cars.

I think we've known what's lost. We drive
interstate to visit extended family for Christmas,

speeding by winter wheat and bison farms.
Bison refuse to be cowed, but the few

families that survived American slaughter
reside on tracts of treeless land that's cloistered

with high-tensile steel. They eat prodigious
sums of grass until a more humane death.

The outcome seems different to us still eating.
I've sometimes wanted to change who we've been,

but our bodies plow toward origin. The prayer
placards lilt along a dormant soy field—*Hail Mary,*

full of grace—we pass at eighty miles per hour—
the Lord is with thee. I wait for the return

of wildness—*Blessed art thou amongst women.*
And blessed is the fruit of thy womb—

a billboard: *Did you defend the unborn?*
You're in my body. Have you observed me

slowing as I accumulate more of you? I must
be more in you, but we've no blessed fruit.

I feel a daring resistance in our physics.
Unlike cattle, the bison can graze in winter,

shoveling ice-topped snow with her muzzle
to root out grasses latent underneath.

Winter Skin

My elbows are eczematous,
inflamed with blisters and rough patches,

and my wife's fingers blanch in the cold,
her vessels constricted, we suspect,

by genes and a smoking mother. We're plaqued
inside and the dead cells pile up,

but it's just discomfort. We watch geese
above a city landfill trading

positions in their V to share
the drag of their travel. My wife claps

and swears and rubs her hands, commanding
fingers pink, and the north side landfill

burns underground—*a smoldering
event*—so pillars of fire eat

gas waste twenty-four seven. The air
irritates there. Becoming smaller

within and larger without, I hand
her my gloves and we drive home,

but our gutter's fallen when we get there.
I don't seek a cause. The three-foot

icicle she asked me to knock down—
a growth *I forgot* to see how long

it'd stall—lies shattered on the driveway,
speckled with clots of frozen leaves.

Bones, Granite, Dirt, and Brains: A Soteriology

Wood siding on my neighbor's home crawls
with silverfish. At night they run the planks

and dive into cracks. I can't see their legs,

just scaled, metallic abdomens that flash
in electric light. They disgust me, their molt,

casting aside whole shells of younger selves,
but I've seen no animal grace with age.

Parked in a leather chair, my grandfather's body

endured long after his mind had moldered,
ringing a brass cowbell, the flat peals for needs

my grandma tended. My brother snatched the bell
once and ran, and I remember the old man's mouth

forming a great lacuna where meaning had been,

but his yelled words decayed in me. The body can
be monument. Bones, granite, dirt, and brains

are filled through with spaces, and I can see
the future if I trace my present bloodline.

My father loses words, a stutter-like stall

of sentence completion. I hear myself
do it sometimes. I try to prepare my wife:

Will you ever be ready for arrant care?
When do I forget diatomaceous earth,

the fossils of hard-shelled algae,

dusted near molt can kill the silverfish?
A younger form of me would have liked a statue

built for his memory, but like everything else
absurd and living, that has passed. Repotting

houseplants for spring with soil we'd bought

the autumn prior, my wife found living worms.
They overwintered in a sack of dirt

we'd stored in the basement, oblivious of what
still writhed within. Some rejected their bright,

new windowsilled homes. Trying to be helpful,

I vacuumed them from the carpet, their sun-crisped
bodies breaking down in transit to a bag

where they amalgamated with our hair,
dead skin, and the domestic dusts we shed.

Wind Farm

Watch the separate hands—three-spoked and churning—
atop their posts, a hundred or more across
this Indiana. They make nothing up there

but friction—sack the drag and drag it down
to our level. Now drive to the pinwheel
point on the highway and watch the turbine line:

white spokes flowering from a single post—
conjoined as though space were a myth. This season
our friends may and will couple daily to serve

water and dirt made prime rib and green beans.
Two become one then five so quickly—*Oops,
an oopsie*—make it six—pop up like mushrooms

that move, eat, drink. Find air, its bulky movement,
the circulation from dense to less dense,
erect these fingered pillars to drive the power

beneath the soybeans, a network of roots
and wires to feed, to clothe and warm. We must
shelter all making, these panoplies of power.

History is Coriolis in bodies
we can see—pressure down on the Puritans,
watch them boat west, against the westerlies,

against the globe's counterclockwise rotation.
Depends which pole you're on. Prevailing winds
prevail in choosing their perspective. The last

summer wedding of this summer's weddings:
a high-pressure system conducts the bride
and groom indoors, though not before *I do*'s.

That can't be a good sign. Inside the tent—
the only dry ground in that field—there's time
for open bar before the taking down—

this up-and-down the ritual—before
guests, stuffed, leave nothing behind since there's nothing
ever misused, and before the couple drives

to a rented room to make the winter full
with one more baby shower. Electrified
soybeans spooned down the easy, wanting mouth—

rub the back until it swallows. *Don't bolt
your food next time.* Relish this movement, feel
it slowly working down the esophagus,

endorphins flushing through the cortex. These cuds
won't need more chewing. *Here, drink some water,*
swallow until it plops into the hardest-

working bile. *Receive the power.* Make
more, *make more.* We have made nothing up
above this besieged plain, our tent-staked homes,

our white and weedlike spires grown thick together
with unclenched fists, the needs coursing it down
to ground we've done with breaking. Listen, it hums.

Transference

The squirrels grow slow this time of year
bearing last-chance acorns across our street.
It's in our nature to denature our dead
for padded boxes, and someone's always saying
how lifelike they look, aren't they. More fact
takes flight in a skyward splash of crows
spilled from the corded mass we left in the road.
You squirmed at the *thump* beneath your tire
and later shivered because everything matters
if you dwell long enough. I tried to divert you
since no one scatters remains anymore—a shame
that boxed people won't touch the earth again—
so I stole blame for distracting you, guilt being
an unsaid thing we vowed to share. All autumn,
our neighbor blows leaves out of his yard
but doesn't bag them. He scatters them
into the street, another gesture, for they'll be
back and in our yard and across the alley
and especially back. Loss is inconvenient,
and yet he works so hard for the luxury
a clear plot of grass confers. Because pain
can enter through the eyes, I look forward
to wintering in the ugly comfort of decay
without you. We have to hope, don't we, the birds
get by some winter on this mess we've made.
Why else uproot saplings but to show the knack
of a singular oak to shade a patch of gravestones.

Ouroboric

From the mist of insects above me, pairs fall like ash
or skin. The small one on my forearm climbs

the backside of the other, which bucks and turns
a circle, snapping after its rear, but he's already in

and clamped to her abdomen. When we fought

yesterday I was wrong and I wasn't and I must
show my wife I'm sorry because the transmutation

of *me* to *me and mine* is material. This family
I met at work donated the father's body but asked

to keep his back skin and the serpentine crest

tattooed across it. Like bickering again about who does
or doesn't do enough housework, repurposing a father's

epidermis as a lampshade heirloom is absurd and not.
The bloodless outer layer of the skin is only one

millimeter thick, so as the female chases him

and thus herself once more, they feel my pulse below.
He tries to exit her but can't—they have to work

together now, clambering apart until they're separate.
But when she charges at him, he's too fast to flight,

leaving her on my arm. Alone, I can follow the blood,

trailing a vessel back to its aorta, but I've yet to capture
with my body all I mean. My wife once asked me,

Why is it we always love the sad song? We came
home from dinner, and I made us drinks. She turned

on an album and lay down on the kitchen hardwood.

I joined her there, feeling nothing beneath my soles,
and when the song came on, she set it for repeat.

The Elephant Rocks

grow sumac in their dirt deposits. Rain-filled
depressions harbor tadpoles and mosquito larvae
    like half-wombs. Hiking boulder to boulder

and slipping through chasms, the space between
    downcut by water like a saw, we are not
alone here. Lichens green the gray-red granite

    in crusts of algo-fungal marriage, and our friends
are getting divorced already. I thought we all agreed
    to spurn our parents' cleaving, though who hasn't

outlived something he believed in? Scientists posit
    the sun, in advanced age, will devour so much fuel
it burns this all to hell. We must rethink the myths

    of our engagement: we committed to consume
each other till we're cold. Had I known my body
    a natural resource, I would've better tended it

for you. Spring peepers animate the path before us,
    so we retreat to barren granite where death is less
probable. These huddled stones, once magmatic,

    weren't always outcrop. Overlying rock abrades
in time, but now the overlying rock, Elephant
    Rocks are conserved from quarrying but exposed

to rain. I want us to begin by seeing everything
    will be exhausted, so on a timeline long enough
no one's jilted. Like the fulsome crop of elephant ears

    that you admired enjoying our healthy distance
from a star, when we start underground we break
    the surface sharing our devotion to the sun.

III.

The Noctambulists

I.

At first you feel very awake. The spring
was dammed, the cave's gush balked
by limestone boulders, water gathering
in a hollow before it swelled the river,
so we dipped into the cold-spring pool.
Submerged to the carotids, I became
sleepwalk inverted, my brain warm
and keen on pain the rest of me numbed from.
You shouldn't wake a sleepwalker
is a myth. She always wakes me.
Once, our bedroom crawled
with spiders, and when I came to,
she kept crying, *Ohmygod, ohmygod*,
and blood ran down my face, her hands,
and one corner of the dresser. Another time,
on a red-flag day, I crept too far
into the ocean and it took me in. The water
sealed my mouth and milled my body
against the sand. You swim and swim
for shore until you finally grasp your body
won't carry you forever. Lifeguards,
three of them with red buoys slung over
their torsos, restored me to the beach air
where, dead-tired, I puked the ocean out.

II.

Bull sharks swim up the Mississippi, singular
in their blood's regulation of salt in freshwater.
The northernmost shark caught on record

was hooked on the Illinois side near the Piasa Bird,
a fish-bird-reptile-deer painted on a bluff
in red-black-green. The Bird Who Devoured Men

whisked people from the riverbanks, one story
tells it, and survivors drew the cryptozoological
nightmare on limestone. My dreams are so

much smaller. After the sightless locomotion,
my brain grasps in the dark for an outer world,
yet I too know to document my fears for memory.

I took her there, where Missouri is a floodplain
and Illinois rises in limestone. We stopped
to see what's left of the beast, the Piasa now

reduced to a roadside attraction, a metal sign
bolted to rock face. We recognize the landmark
by its plight against decline, and it's by them

she's ever found her way. Like a graveyard,
the gravel parking lot adjacent was crowded
with Queen Anne's lace and abandoned trailers.

III.

This is the one where you wake up in the mirror
with your neck elongated and the light yellow.

You sit on the toilet, remembering a goose

with fur that stilted across the frozen pond
in our park. *Buy me dinner*, it begged, its neck

writhing animatronically. You ran away,

past the flowering magnolias, and you flush
because you have to see your body again.

In the mirror, your neck is less serpentine

now and more natural, though there's less of you,
but the heart—*Where's your heart, friend?*—

still pounds, and somehow the excess

cervical vertebrae were never yours
to keep. Her voice calls from the bedroom.

You can't go back. Instead you believe

in her body beyond the light, so you grope
her feet through the blanket and trace them

up to her waist. When she moans some

and turns her back to you, you're satisfied
it's her because you've felt this all before.

IV.

The question with cryonics is never
Can we cure his disease? but *How in hell
will we revive him?* Asleep four days,
Lazarus woke with the new problems
of walking with his feet and hands bound
with linen and his eyes covered with cloth.
Today if I slept four days I'd wake
connected to an IV and many machines.
To prevent information-theoretic death,
the last and newest of the deaths,
we vitrify the cells, but *cryopreserved*
holds more water than *dead*. Anything can
go if you find a way to see your way
beyond the light. On April First,
Wisconsin men discovered in a cold spring
a bull shark, near-frozen and drowsing
inside a sunken pickup. Who has never
found himself trespassing? You could
say slowing its circulation prevented
the shark from losing salt. You could call it
comatose or ask how the shark got there
or if it ever was. Given what you've learned
about the limits of your body, you may ask
yourself why you believed the story true
only because someone said it was so.

V.

The problem with the underworld
is that I didn't know how many days

I was dead or that I even was,
which is not unrelated. Orpheus

at least knew where he was going.
Well past the somatic and metabolic deaths,

Eurydice's only hope for resurrection
was O's refusal of her social end.

Whose hope? What a trip to see her there,
playing chess with your grandmother,

and suspect you aren't asleep but
maybe were. Believe me you'll want to

beat the daylights out of the man
holding her under. That feeling's older

than any of your blood. But O understood:
best to forget the *why*s and *how*s.

Even the *what*s. To surface her, you
train your eyes on light that shimmers

overhead. Then kick like hell.

VI.

From the stern, I saw the bloom of moon jellyfish
floating the surface in every way. Even if their tentacles

are short and their sting weak and the captain keeps a bottle
of vinegar aboard, you jump into negative space

then swim hard for the bottom. The jellyfish buoyed vivid
and unknowable in that shallow water, like the blinking

red lights of a wind farm at night, me driving the interstate
while she slept. I watched the turbines' red-light constellation

seem to shift as I drove us home—there, then black,
red dots, then nothing—but it was us changing in space.

There's almost comfort underwater, that everything
is pushing in on your body but you can let nothing out.

She plunged in behind me, and I motioned the way.
With fins and masks, we could move fast and like we belonged.

Moon jellyfish pulsate and eat, and *They'll only hurt you
if you fail to keep your distance.* Being alien is something

you feel. Without their beacons, how else could I have known
the three-spoked power machines were out there? We surfaced

beyond the bloom, exhilarated with oxygen and waning of the fear
we'd never get alone, and when we found the reef, we didn't touch.

VII.

On a boat near the first Piasa,
both paint and limestone bluff gone,
quarried for lime a century ago,
we watch the Asian carp

go mad for the motor's whine.
They leap in hordes, slamming
their bony flanks against
the river surface. In this one,

I kick the boat into gear, but one carp
lands on the bow by her feet
and bursts, splattering blood
across her legs. One, skyborne,

knocks her to her knees. Another ribbons
across the bow, and another,
and more, and so I wake, bailing
meat and bones from the boat

and scooping her body from the bed
because I vowed to her. *Let me go*
—*who are you?* The dark is familiar,
but often silence is how I sense return,

not *You're scaring me* and a palm
to my jaw. There was that awful
distance between O and E—
he looks back, him alive and her

still dead and never not dead again.
I descend the basement stairs.
The sleepwalker is safest
in his own bed, his own home, possibly

alone. There's nothing E can say
that O can use on the other side.
I scour the basement for things
I know—the suitcases, the litter box,

some garden tools. Beneath the stairs,
I find a bag of mortar and blood
in my mouth. I lift the bag and
make it weigh me still. If not

for the bandages, could Lazarus
have rolled the stone away himself?
The floor is cracked and dry
where the bag was. Without a barrier

between, the mortar drew moisture
from the floor, so you're left
with a bag of cement and one
more crack in your foundation.

VIII.

Outliving social death, the cryopreserved man
is free to smile over the photos and trinkets

in his storage locker. He listens to hours
of his voice he recorded before vitrification.

The noctambulist, mourned but thought alive,
forever comes to. One day you wake up

to a bullfrog croaking and geese by the pond
and the magnolias bloomed, and you are

walking past the park bench where you proposed.
The body is yours, you know, but the bench is

winter-worn more than you recall, and when
did the magnolias bloom? You ask if she knows

this landmark or about the blooms, but she hasn't
answered any of your questions for as long

as you can remember, which isn't very long.
Resurrection day for the cryopreserved man

can be celebrated only if he finds someone
he knew who forgets time. *Oh, was I asleep?*

Maybe he begins to understand himself reborn.
Here's the one where the noctambulist comes to

while looking into his wife's eyes, and having
been dead before, he sees she cannot see him.

IX.

I nightsweat. The sleepwalk is not
contagious, but even if they lie parallel,
so much passes between two bodies
sharing a bed most nights. The Orphics
believed we could, by purification
and ritual, free ourselves from our evil
natures through each cycle of life.
When I wake with damp sheets
and wet hair and there's still no light,
I change clothes and she sleeps through.
If you can't keep sleeping, you're just
walking, and even if nighttime passes
faster than day, who can wait for it?
During a storm, I trudged down
to the basement and found a foot
of standing water, the rain rushing
under the cellar door and burbling up
the sewer drains, too full and too much
outside to take the water away. I went back
to bed and listened for the end of rain.
After you sleep, you wake to a new kind
of your body, and that morning, I found
the water gone and a sediment
fanning across the floor in waves.

X.

I've been watching you change. I pretend
to sleep while you dress for work,

and when you pull on your underwear,
I still want to rise and throw you

on the bed because if you could feel
my weight, maybe I could stop being history.

You're scaring me. Lazarus was mostly
socially dead but probably comatose

because for all we know the dead
must raise themselves. In our park,

did you see, the magnolias bloomed?
I collected some of the waxy green leaves

because I remember you wanted to make
a wreath and today I found them in the trash.

Daylight how it is, we sleep in shifts,
so people take each other's place. Maybe

you presumed me dead, but it doesn't change
how much you're in the mirror now

when you know I'm not asleep. Like riptide,
if you don't make a landmark of the sun,

you can get turned around in there.
Timing and space are always everything.

It was far too late when I learned you
don't fight the undertow. You still must swim

your heart out, but instead of thrashing against
the tide you swim along the waves, accepting

the longer path near-parallel to shore.

XI.

We sort through sopping cardboard boxes,
drying what can be salvaged and restoring it
in plastic bins. I sweep the dried sediment,
and she's behind me on her hands and knees,
scrubbing bleach-water on the cement floor
and stone walls and anything the water touched.
O's tragedy isn't that he thought anyone
could save anyone but that he wasn't prepared
to be dead. I'm not ready to blame him.
Another young man drowned in the river this week,
the water up, and no one knows how long
he was under, but that's the question, isn't it.
The other question must always be how long
did he struggle, the river drawing heat
and fight and flight from his skin till he's empty.
There are limits to what we think can be
resurrected. It's different for everyone,
how long you can live underwater,
and given what we've learned from fear,
rescuers don't approach the drowner head on.
Later there might be time for the *hows* and *whats*
or *whys*, but you will always have to cure first death
if you want to stay awake. Here is the one
where I trekked upstream thinking I could reach
some sort of spring but found the river basin-fed.
Oh, was I sleeping? I try to keep my eyes open
through the chlorine, but she's nowhere near done,
so I open the cellar door and carry a trash bag, heavy
with our water-damaged things, out to the dumpster.

IV.

Shape-Shifter

Breakneck and blood-full inside
my skull, I hike the tor and find
solution pans still half-filled
with last week's rain. Stagnant water
corrodes the rock with its weak acids,
its frost wedging, and from a fracture
in the granite a blue-tailed skink bolts.
With the low pH of your *without*
puddling across my cortex, I have to
unsettle. I chase the lizard down
the south rock face until it stops.
We take each other in. The blue-tailed
skink can loose its tail, the limb writhing
a distraction for the predator,
because in our morphology of need,
some body can be discarded
to preserve the body. Beneath us, lichen
speckle the rock, alga and fungus
two organisms slow-grown
to indistinct, yet they weather
the granite they cling to. We were told,
Keep this place beautiful. Do you believe me
there aren't shape-shifters, only the declining
shapes our bodies make? I thought I understood
you must be skull-like, both whole
and inextricable, but there's no knowing
how or if until I find out where you end now.
Even if it looks that way, a body can't replace itself
with itself. The blue-tailed skink is brilliant
only once, but the tail that grows back brown
is harder to spot against the mud and stone.

Self-Portrait with Asian Carp and Mississippi

Trees on the bluff, its layered limestone
    and the plants grown into rockface,
        down to the river road and in

across two pontoons and the water
    you stand in. Try to make the image
        wash you out. You take on the sun's halo,

the colors shading toward the limit
    of your retinas, but if you document the light
        scorching across your cortex when alone,

you may never displace her *I'm sorry*s
    on the kitchen floor or all the scenes
        you never saw but have. You leave her

and everyone on the sandbar to walk until the mud
    receives your kneecaps. The river's never clear,
        but Asian carp are probably feeding

in this meander, the takers taking, never filling,
    though they deplete. We finally see infestation
        in death of a species that never had a chance

to adapt. You trace it back to some mistake,
    like anyone can know a thing before it is,
        could see what she submerged. You can't

eradicate what's bred this long, but you knew
    that bodies in a place they don't belong
        can turn invasive. The fish are made visible

by what they feel: a passing speedboat
    tears a seam in the river, and from the motor-whine
      and wake, dozens of Asian carp

          leap into the sun, their mouths wide open.

Tor

Acid from lichen, the green skin patching
across the stone, eats away at what remains after the quarry.
Beside, what was more boulder now is green
water more deep than broad. Black oaks around the pit root wide
across the shallow, granitic soil and down,

aggravating stress fractures in the stone. Everything is breaking
and also breaking. The clouds southwest
approach gravid with rain—everywhere decomposing—
but not even water can outlast the sun. I take
a fragment of the gray-red granite home. I scatter. This skeleton

that holds me up disintegrates, and though
short-lived, the black oak survives a couple decades longer
than I might. Raccoons, bobwhite,
the blue-tailed skinks—its branches and hollows bear many lives,
but more inhabit the black oak laid supine.

Flood Map

I wake to my arm asleep and the rain. A story
beneath me, water's flowing up the drains

and under the cellar door and running rivulets
down the white stone walls, but this is a problem

I don't know until I descend the stairs and find
the foot-deep dark spanning across my basement.

Water inside can't go away until the water
outside is gone because there can be order,

even in so much water, like how the needling pain
must come before the arm's mine again to use.

All this will recede and then be the worst flood
since last year's 100-year flood. My river city

builds more and higher levees, which don't stop
floods but shirk them elsewhere because some problems

are only your problems if you don't prevent them.
Under the bridge, someone in a johnboat

will document this crest on the concrete columns
with stripes of orange spray paint. The flood maps

will be redrawn. Anyone raised on rivers knows
nothing can stay the way they found it, but

this is another thing I learned again before I knew
I had forgotten. Like how the water's bound

to nothing but itself and Earth and yet we will
never not be bound to it, or that a flood is just a river

bigger than you're used to, but also sometimes
the problem was yours before you were conscious

it existed. I salvage some boxes, and when nothing's left
to do tonight, I can finally feel sick that I keep cleaning up

tomorrow. Pattern seeking, like mapmaking, must be
inexorable and absurd. I return to my story and lie

in bed next to the woman I married, and despite the blood
and feeling back in my hands, I cannot touch her.

Salvage: A Field Guide

Snow weighs on upholstered chairs in the alley.
    My neighbor returns each dusk with a truckload
        of things to fill his garage. Like how Earth

maintains a relatively steady mass
    regardless of space dust subsumed, gases lost,
        or what was birthed or died on a given rotation,

each load replaces other matter. One
    magenta hamper with a plunger handle
        sticking out, a yellowed recycling bin,

and two mirrors overwinter. What he abandons
    to the alley waits for garbage men on Tuesdays
        or other pickers cruising alleys in their flatbeds.

On the south side of the streets, snow melts
    slower here due to axial tilt, and our home's
        south face admits the most light, so it's there

I tend my wife's air plants. Some rootless,
    others nothing but bracteate fists, they subsist
        on sunlight, baths, and domestic debris.

Although I am attentive, their green fades.
    Osage orange trees in the park aren't autochthons
        either, yet they thrive. Prized for shelterbelt

before barbwire, *Maclura pomifera*
    grows just fine here—plenty of yellow-green,
        tuberculated fruits peek through the snow.

Squirrels filch the seeds, discarding rinds and a flesh
    that poisons insects and people, the fruit assured
        a leisurely rot or composting by the park staff.

To break down and nurture another organism
       is one way to live forever. These female trees
              don't bear saplings without humans

calculating it so, and her air plants won't pup
       if I don't buy fluorescent lamps to complement
              the sun. Once in motion, an object can persist

beyond its element. Someone dumped wooden pallets
       on the alley pile, the mass begetting mass
              the way a landfill revegetates with wildflowers.

Zygo-

With a handful of your hair
gathered from the bathroom floor

and a spider stranded in the tub,
I watch me feel my zygomatic arch

in the mirror and how when you're not here
you are. These awful keratins,

the last dead cells pulsing from our bodies
even underneath the earth, I hold your body

in my hand, and there's so much
I can live without—one kidney, a few pints

of blood, some liver. How many legs
the spider? Replacement and regeneration

are all but the same way of giving form
to loss. I trace the cheekbone

back to the temporal because every body
is a mirror here where the air is thick

and water's far from scarce, where we are
always a little incomplete. I hold

your body in my body, but if I believe
in a finitude of skin, even its frantic give

and take, what more can I accept?
What can't I sever? Hair grows slower

at night. When I wake sweat-soaked,
blood-thumping and you're not here, I push

ten fingers down on the zygomata
to make sure I am. Another winter night

I joined you at the tub ledge and we warmed
our feet. Side by side, we looked past

the steam and our silhouettes reflected
to watch the blood returning to our toes.

7-10 Years

There's nothing left of your skeleton
from the day we met. Every cell
forming your spinal column, your femurs
and scapulae, has been replaced.
Your blood traversed the thousand miles
of your body and died in your spleen
again and again, and I'm sorry
I never saw you change. I haven't
touched any of the skin you have
today because there's nothing left
of your liver from the first night
you didn't come home. You said, *I can't
recognize this person I am,*
but none of me was me either. Look
at all the dead skin we surrender
to our beds. Replacement isn't clean
exchange. We don't know if we'll be
stuck with our cortices, the shame-store
of our amygdalae, so when
I trace a suture where my young
skull bones fuse, what I can't let go of
is if we want to change the people
we have been, we don't have to.

Nonunion

Older than anyone alive
        we know by blood, the oak
                behind our house is losing limbs.

How better to learn balance
        than the tree's shrewd arithmetic
                of branch and root. When we wrap

our arms around the trunk,
        we cannot touch each other, and yet
                we know the earth's reclaiming

roots beneath our feet. I used to
        believe in the promise of our bones
                —to never break, or that the stone

of my body, once fractured, would
        always reunite. I used to know
                you were there, reaching for me.

Like the small bone in my hand
        that lost its blood supply, we can't
                predict where death will come from,

only that what is dying can hurt us.
        What was it you believed in? No one
                will blame us for salvaging a house

from the burden of this oak tree,
        and yet, if you could speak to me,
                I swear on what phloem is left

pulsing between us, I'll stay however long
        you need to feel the branches fall.

Self-Portrait with Fescue and Dogwood

When the acorn hailed down on my scalp, I was spreading a
    grass seed too blue.

When the blood reached my forehead, I crammed the oak seed
    into the vessel.

A man once carried a spider alive beneath his skin for days,
    the spider burrowing from bellybutton to heart, and
    no less than four hundred microflora luxuriate in my gut.

Some things live everywhere.

The phlebotomist said I have skinny veins—she said they roll.

Not much grows in the dirt before my house but maybe green
    perennial leaves if I'm vigilant.

How much seed have I cast?

When social death didn't always follow somatic death,
    undertakers tied the dead man to a bell, the string
    a taut umbilical cord that coupled plot and the
    undertaker's home.

It isn't that I'm sick of my huge heart shoving this blood
    through narrow vessels.

I say I have no grave mycological concerns, but when my dust
    and bone chips pour into the dirt, I expect a hound's
    tree to take root above.

If the berries taste bitter, at least they're edible.

It's that I'm tired of hunting other bodies for what I'm missing
    in myself.

When the xylem pulses earth and water into the sky, finally
    I circulate.

Pathology

Our house can't hold onto the sun, its brick
seeping more heat each day. The winter
we moved in, we found a bat above

the kitchen sink. We brought it down
in a painter's tarp, so it woke and panicked
against the see-through plastic. We ran out back

to the deck and tossed the bundle, leaving it
all day while we painted and cleaned.
At dusk, I stirred the tarp with a broom,

and the bat was gone and you were pleased
awhile. On the coldest nights, when the furnace
couldn't keep up and the black vasculature

nearest our skin shut out our blood, we warmed
the outer reaches of our bodies in each other.
I knew cold is absence but had to learn heat

is a process, sometimes borne by blood,
and may be finally understanding you
aren't coming back. All this time I've begged you

to open your body and give voice to the everything
you've stored there, convinced we could
be cured by the expulsion and somehow stop

the shame and fear from vibrating back
across the tool-shaped bones of our middle ears.
That first New Year's Day we climbed into

the attic looking for a place to keep our Christmas
decorations and found the colony of bats, dozens
of still, brown bodies huddled in hibernation

and hanging from the exposed brick chimney.
They'd always been there. We agreed to leave
the bats to their roost, but when they moved on

that spring, I scraped up dried dung piles
from the plywood floor while you sealed off
every crack in the attic you could find.

Exposure Being: A Letter

The campsite clerk said give myself some distance
from the river. *We flash-flood here—the clay*

doesn't soak up rain fast enough. The whole way down,
cumulonimbi hung and shortleaf pines lined

the state highway like skinny shelterbelt.
No wind yet, it's so hot I start to wish

you were here but can't because I fear you are.
I saw seven dead armadillos on the shoulder,

the husk of one getting picked at by a crow,
but I don't put faith in signs or forecasts

until they're true. I'm here to feel my body separate
from your body and let you do with yours

what you will. If it's going to rain, I want the rain.
Nine-banded armadillos weren't always in Missouri,

and plated shells notwithstanding, they can't hear
or see much so we say they're ill-suited

for the highways, but it's you who taught me
I can't know what anything is like to any body

but mine. Like when you drove home drunk again
and said, *I don't want to be alive anymore,*

what did you mean? When I say I saw many
metal-sided churches off the highway,

each with a proclamation and a smattering
of gravestones in the field next door, I want you

to know sometimes I can feel all the awful
weight of when this ends before it does.

This *what* is worthless, though, without the *when*
and *how*. I don't want to be here, but I staked my tent

by the shallow river and maybe thunderstorm
is how I get what I came for, exposure being

one proven way to feel the limits of my skin.
I'm afraid I won't get clear of you while you are

using your body, but what happens if you die
before we're apart? Where could you go?

Near dusk, I walked the one-lane bridge
over the river and lay down in the middle

so I could see over the side. I found my reflection first
but then saw sky behind me and the undersides

of sycamores along the bank and, soon enough,
the bed stones underneath the current.